100 COMMON BIRD CALLS in EAST AFRICA

DAVE RICHARDS
BRIAN FINCH

DEDICATION

To the dedicated conservationists of East Africa,
all of whom are integral in guaranteeing that tomorrow
we can still enjoy a dawn chorus!

Published by Struik Nature
(an imprint of Penguin Random House South Africa (Pty) Ltd)
Reg. No. 1953/000441/07
Estuaries No. 4, Oxbow Crescent,
Century Avenue, Century City, 7441
PO Box 1144, Cape Town, 8000 South Africa

Visit **www.randomstruik.co.za** and join the
Struik Nature Club for updates, news,
events and special offers.

1 3 5 7 9 10 8 6 4 2

Publisher: Pippa Parker
Managing editor: Helen de Villiers
Editor: Emily Bowles
Designer: Neil Bester

Reproduction by Hirt & Carter Cape (Pty) Ltd
Printed and bound by Toppan Leefung Packaging and Printing (Dongguan) Co., Ltd. China

Print 978 1 77584 251 4
E-PUB 978 1 77584 252 1
E-PDF 978 1 77584 253 8

MIX
Paper from
responsible sources
FSC® C104723

CONTENTS

INSIDE BACK COVER –
CD WITH 100 BIRD CALLS

INTRODUCTION TO BIRD CALLS

Bird sounds are all around us, in the bush, on safari, in our gardens and even in towns and cities: in the bush, we may hear the calls of Helmeted Guineafowl or the iconic sound of the African Fish Eagle; in our gardens, it may be the duet of Tropical Boubous or the melodious liquid whistles of a Black-headed Oriole; in our cities we hear the screams of Little Swifts as they fly in tight flocks around their nesting sites, or the calls of Yellow-billed Kites high in the sky.

The best time to hear birds is when large numbers sing, soon after dawn, in what is known as the 'dawn chorus'. Birds call at this time because sounds travel best in the cool morning air. Their calls or songs are used to attract mates or to claim territory. Some birds also mimic the songs of other birds – the Rüppell's Robin Chat is a good example. Why they do this is still a subject of much discussion. There are far more different bird calls than there are different types of bird. Some birds have a beautiful song, like the Grey-capped Warbler. Others have harsh, unmusical voices, such as the Pied Crow or the Hadada Ibis.

Sometimes birds are easy to locate because they sing from prominent positions; others are more secretive. Rufous-naped Larks, for instance, sing from the tops of bushes or from fence posts, and African Pied Wagtails are easily spotted and seem to sing at any time of the day; people in rural villages often regard them as bringing good luck. The Grey-capped Warbler, by contrast, sings while hidden in a bush – only its distinctive calls betray its presence. Similarly, the Red-chested Cuckoo is common, but difficult to see.

This book and the accompanying CD bring together some of the most common and interesting bird sounds that may be heard in East Africa. If you have only recently become interested in birds, you might like to start by listening to the CD and familiarising yourself with the calls of those birds that you often see in your environment. In time you'll come to recognise more calls and be able to identify even more birds by ear.

Tropical Boubous (left) are known for their duets; their bell-like whistles have earned them the popular alternative name 'bell birds'. Grey-capped Warblers (right) have a sweet and varied repertoire. They too are known for duetting.

HOW TO USE THIS BOOK

- The book includes a photograph and some information on each of the 100 birds featured. It tells you where to find them, if they are in the region all year or if they are only visiting, and what they eat. A distribution map appears for each of the species, showing where in the region the bird occurs.

- The CD provides the name of each bird and its call or calls. Use the CD with the book to match the pictures of the birds with the sounds they make.
- As you learn and remember the sounds, you will be able to look for those birds when you hear them: simply follow the call and look for the bird that's making it.

CD track number and common name of bird.

Common name in Swahili

The distribution map shows the parts of East Africa in which the bird can be seen.

Look out for the icons that indicate food and nesting information.

Information about the call and the corresponding track number can be found at the bottom of the pages. Some tracks feature more than one sound, each of which is described.

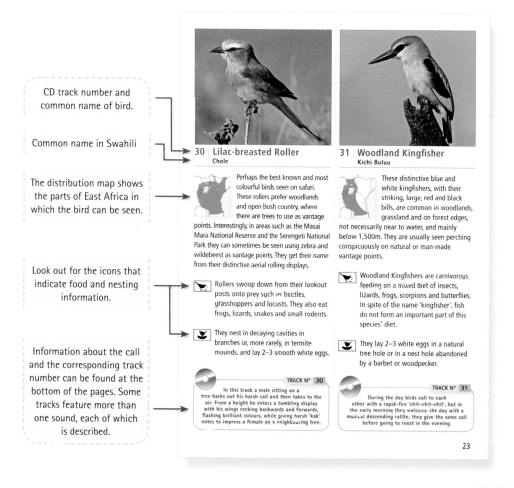

30 | Lilac-breasted Roller
Chole

Perhaps the best known and most colourful birds seen on safari. These rollers prefer woodlands and open bush country, where there are trees to use as vantage points. Interestingly, in areas such as the Masai Mara National Reserve and the Serengeti National Park they can sometimes be seen using zebra and wildebeest as vantage points. They get their name from their distinctive aerial rolling displays.

Rollers swoop down from their lookout posts onto prey such as beetles, grasshoppers and locusts. They also eat frogs, lizards, snakes and small rodents.

They nest in decaying cavities in branches or, more rarely, in termite mounds, and lay 2–3 smooth white eggs.

TRACK N° 30

In this track a male sitting on a tree barks out his harsh call and then takes to the air. From a height he enters a tumbling display with his wings rocking backwards and forwards, flashing brilliant colours, while giving harsh 'kak' notes to impress a female on a neighbouring tree.

31 | Woodland Kingfisher
Kichi Buluu

These distinctive blue and white kingfishers, with their striking, large, red and black bills, are common in woodlands, grassland and on forest edges, not necessarily near to water, and mainly below 1,500m. They are usually seen perching conspicuously on natural or man-made vantage points.

Woodland Kingfishers are carnivorous, feeding on a mixed diet of insects, lizards, frogs, scorpions and butterflies. In spite of the name 'kingfisher', fish do not form an important part of this species' diet.

They lay 2–3 white eggs in a natural tree hole or in a nest hole abandoned by a barbet or woodpecker.

TRACK N° 31

During the day birds call to each other with a rapid-fire 'chit-chit-chit', but in the early morning they welcome the day with a musical descending rattle; they give the same call before going to roost in the evening.

23

TIPS FOR LISTENING TO BIRD CALLS

Try to notice:

- whether there are any non-vocal elements in the song, such as 'drumming' with the bill
- the number of birds that are singing
- how long the song is
- whether there is any repetition
- the speed of the song, and
- whether the pitch is high, low or variable.

Answering these questions will help to attune your ear, and it may be useful to take notes. You should soon find yourself remembering and recognising more and more bird calls – and hopefully increasing your enjoyment of nature.

Rüppell's Robin-Chats are excellent mimics – even experienced birders may struggle to recognise the singer's true identity.

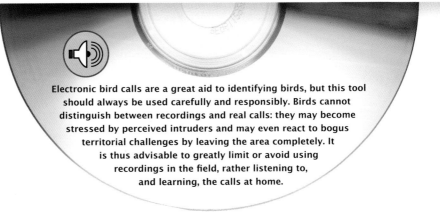

Electronic bird calls are a great aid to identifying birds, but this tool should always be used carefully and responsibly. Birds cannot distinguish between recordings and real calls: they may become stressed by perceived intruders and may even react to bogus territorial challenges by leaving the area completely. It is thus advisable to greatly limit or avoid using recordings in the field, rather listening to, and learning, the calls at home.

Enjoy getting to know your local birds!

1 | Helmeted Guineafowl
Kanga

Helmeted Guineafowl are well-known birds that occur in flocks, except when breeding. They are most active at dawn and dusk, and are often found bathing in dust to dislodge parasites and get rid of excess preen oil. Very vocal at times, they are particularly noisy if a predator is spotted. At night they roost in trees, but will also fly up into trees if threatened. Guineafowl are resident throughout the year.

 These birds feed mostly on seeds, but also eat berries and insects.

 They make a scrape nest during the rainy season, usually located under a bush, and lay about 6–8 yellow to pale brown eggs with darker spotting.

2 | Yellow-necked Spurfowl
Kwale Shingonjano

Yellow-necked Spurfowl are fairly common in savanna country. They are usually found in pairs or small family parties, and individuals are often seen perched on a low branch or on top of a bush or termite mound. As resident birds, they stay in the region throughout the year.

 They feed mostly on seeds and are often found scratching through elephant dung, looking for undigested seeds.

 The nest is a scrape in the ground, usually located under a bush or in dense grass, in which 3–8 (but usually 5) cream or pale pinkish eggs are laid.

3 | Egyptian Goose
Bata Buykini

These are common birds, usually found in pairs near to water, although they also feed in flocks in open areas away from water. At times they can be very vocal, especially when defending their territory. Mainly resident, some Egyptian Geese do wander to take up residence in temporary pools.

Their diet consists of young grass and seeds.

These birds often take over nests abandoned by birds of prey, and they quite often nest inside or on top of a Hamerkop's nest. They may also nest high up on cliff ledges, in hollow trees and sometimes in thick vegetation close to water. They conceal 5–11 cream eggs in a nest, usually made of feathers and down.

4 | Hadada Ibis
Kwarara Hijani

Hadada Ibises are common, familiar residents. Small flocks forage in swamps, marshes and flooded areas on the edges of lakes, in pastureland and in large, suburban gardens. They roost communally, but their nests are solitary.

They feed mainly on insects but also eat small reptiles.

The nest is a loose platform of sticks and twigs, lined with lichens and grass. They lay 2–3 buff or pale olive green eggs, with heavy red-brown blotches and spots.

TRACK N° **03**

Pairs are very territorial – they trumpet loudly when an intruder arrives, then take off in flight, calling as they chase the interloper away.

TRACK N° **04**

Pairs stay in contact with a very loud, distinctive 'ha-haaaa-haaa' call. This probably plays a role in pair bonding and lets other Hadadas know that their territory is occupied.

Hamerkops build big messy nests.

5 | Hamerkop
Fundichuma (Msingwe)

These common birds with their distinctive hammer-shaped heads are found near swamps, shallow lakes and recently flooded areas. Usually they occur singly or in pairs, but larger groups are found along the shores of Lake Victoria. Hamerkops are often very vocal. They are resident birds, but may travel to recently flooded areas and coastal lagoons.

Their diet comprises fish, tadpoles, frogs and, occasionally, small rodents. They typically feed by shuffling a foot in mud or shallow water to disturb their prey.

Male and female may take up to 6 months to build a massive nest, with a small entrance hole, using mainly sticks (a particular nest was found to contain 8,000 sticks), mud and reeds, but also adding odd items such as old clothing and bits of leather, skin or bone. The nest is built in the fork of a tree, usually overhanging water, but is sometimes built on a cliff. The female lays 3–5 chalky white eggs, which soon become stained. These nests are often taken over by Egyptian Geese and occasionally by Grey Kestrels or Barn Owls, which may even evict the occupants.

TRACK N° **05**

This bird looks like a small stork (although it isn't), but its call is more strident and excitable than a stork's. In this clip, a bird arrives at the nest to take over parental duties; the adults greet each other ceremonially, bobbing and bowing, with their crests fully expanded.

6 | Yellow-billed Kite
Mwewe Domonjano

Common in towns and cities throughout their range, Yellow-billed Kites are often seen circling high in the sky before swooping down to seize an item of food. They are resident in the region throughout the year.

These kites are mainly scavengers and feed on insects, especially termites, as well as rodents, lizards and young birds. They will even take domestic chickens that are not protected.

They build a platform of sticks, sometimes containing rubbish, which is well hidden high up in a tree – often a eucalyptus. Here they lay 2–3, but occasionally 4, dull white eggs that may have brown spots and blotches.

TRACK N° **06**

The high-pitched, mewing, 'pii-yorrr' call is a familiar sound around most of the region's larger settlements.

7 | African Fish Eagle
Tai Mlasamki

Found throughout East Africa near rivers, lakes, dams and estuaries, African Fish Eagles are usually seen perched high in a tree. These are resident birds with well-defined territories. They have roughened soles on their feet, which help them hold onto wet, slippery fish.

They eat mostly fish, but also rodents, young egrets and herons, coots and flamingos.

They make a sizeable stick nest at the top of a large tree, usually near water. The female lays and incubates 2, but sometimes as many as 3, white eggs.

TRACK N° **07**

Three sounds are heard on this track: Firstly, members of a pair call from their nest prior to fishing – they're warning other African Fish Eagles that intruders are not welcome. Secondly, immature birds try out their wings from the safety of the nest, giving strange whistling and barking calls. Lastly, the adults cement their bond with protracted echoing calls and a tumbling display over the water.

8 | African Harrier-Hawk
Kipanga-Marungi

 African Harrier-Hawks are common residents that favour woodlands, forests and well-treed city suburbs. They are often seen hanging awkwardly in trees as they search crevices and weavers' nests for prey, with their wings flapping and outspread. They fly slowly, with measured wing beats, often gliding, and twist their tail as they manoeuvre between trees. Occasionally they are seen foraging for prey on the ground.

 Their varied diet includes birds, lizards, snakes, bats, small rodents and insects.

 These birds build a large nest of sticks high up in the fork of a tall tree. The female lays 2–3 buffy-cream eggs, with rich red-brown spots and blotches, at 3-day intervals.

TRACK N° 08
Even when the bird cannot be seen, its call is loud, penetrating and carries. Juveniles that still depend on their parents for food maintain a similar loud, plaintive, single, upslurred call for much of the day and never seem satisfied enough to stop calling.

9 | African Goshawk
Kipanga Misitu

 African Goshawks are fairly common residents in highland forests, woodlands and treed suburban gardens, although they can be difficult to see. They are usually noticed in display flight while it is still fairly dark: they soar high over a forest with rapid fluttering wing beats, followed by a short glide, uttering their call. They are also seen as they dash through the trees in pursuit of their prey.

 Their diet comprises mostly birds but occasionally small rodents, lizards and insects.

 Their nest is a small platform of sticks high in a large tree, in which they lay 2–3 bluish-green eggs.

TRACK N° 09
Their call, which sounds like a louder version of a Bulbul's typical call, is a spaced 'krit-krit-krit', usually uttered in flight. This is a very familiar call in the early morning in well-wooded city gardens, but people often don't know what is making the noise. A search of the sky will reveal the bird flying in circles over its territory.

10 | Augur Buzzard
Shakivale Mweupe

11 | White-bellied Bustard
Tandawala Tumbojeupe

 Augur Buzzards are common residents in the highlands but also occur in low country with isolated hills. They perch on fence posts or dead trees and are often also seen soaring and hovering in strong winds or updrafts from hills. Melanistic (all-black) individuals occur in the highlands.

 They feed on rodents, moles, birds, snakes and insects and also, unfortunately, occasionally eat chickens, for which reason local people often persecute them.

 These buzzards build a stick nest in a tree in which they lay 1–3 bluish-white eggs with sparse brown streaks.

 These are probably the most common bustards seen on safari. They occur in open grasslands and savanna below 2,000m and are usually found in pairs or in family parties. The males are particularly distinctive with a bright blue-grey neck, a white face with black markings and a bright red bill. Bustards rarely fly. When walking, they move their head backwards and forwards. White-bellied Bustards are resident year-round.

 Seeds, insects and spiders are their favoured foods.

 Their nest is a simple scrape on bare ground, often near or under a bush or small tree. The female lays 1–3 (but usually 2) pale olive eggs with grey-brown blotches.

TRACK N° **10**

These birds call together as part of a regular display, often while flying extremely close to each other. In this track, a member of a pair gives a 'rawk–rawk–rawk' from the air, and its perched mate then flies up to join it, responding with the same call.

TRACK N° **11**

In the early morning the grasslands ring with the far-carrying 'kuk-kaatuk' calls these birds give to stay in contact. If a male answers with the same calls, the master of that piece of land barks out a challenge to the potential trespasser.

12 | Common Moorhen
Kukuziwa

Fairly common residents in freshwater lakes with floating and fringing vegetation, among which they submerge themselves when hunting. When walking along the water's edge they have a distinctive, high-stepping gate and often flick their tail, revealing the white undertail. Sometimes they climb up into reeds. These moorhens are found singly, in pairs or in family groups.

 Their diet consists of the seeds and fruits of aquatic plants, as well as insects and tadpoles.

 The saucer-shaped nest is usually built in tall reeds, but, occasionally, in overhanging vegetation, into which the female lays 3–9 creamish-white eggs with red-brown spots or blotches.

TRACK N° 12

When a bird sees an unwanted rival or a potential predator it gives a rapid 'teek' call. In feeding or in display, the call given is a more musical cackle.

13 | Grey Crowned Crane
Mana Taji

Grey Crowned Cranes are fairly common residents in swamps, grasslands and along lake edges. When not breeding they can at times be found in large flocks. Pairs often perform an elaborate dancing display with head bobbing, bowing, mutual preening and leaps into the air; this display is also performed when they are gathered in flocks. Unfortunately these birds are endangered.

 These cranes enjoy eating the seed heads of sedges and grasses as well as frogs, lizards and various invertebrates, including insects. They will also eat cultivated grains.

 The nest is a bulky pile of sedges and grasses made by stamping down the marsh vegetation in shallow water. They lay 1–4 pale blue eggs, which are soon stained by the damp vegetation.

TRACK N° 13

Individual birds trumpet a loud 'o-wahng, o-wahng' to each other at a swamp as a prelude to display. They follow this up with a few circuits, while both birds call together.

14 | Crowned Plover
Ndoero Kibandiko

15 | Speckled Pigeon
Njiwa-Madoa

 Usually found in pairs or groups in areas of short grass, these plovers can be highly territorial: they swoop on intruders and are very vocal when other birds and even mammals approach their area, especially if they have eggs or chicks. Crowned Plovers are resident but will move to areas that provide seasonal food.

 Speckled Pigeons normally occur in rocky habitats and feed in the open, but are increasingly found in villages and towns. They usually occur in pairs, but form large flocks when not breeding. They are very fast flyers, often making loud claps with their wings.

 Their diet consists mainly of insects such as beetles and grasshoppers, which are often gleaned from the dung of large mammals.

 They eat seeds, small fruits and figs, and will also feed on crops.

 The nest is a scrape or a natural depression in (often stony) ground, lined with bits of dead grass, pebbles and even dung from small mammals. They lay 2–3, occasionally 4, pale buff eggs well-camouflaged with blotches and darker 'scribbles'.

 Their nest is a platform of sticks on a rocky ledge or tall building, in which 1–3 chalky white eggs are laid.

TRACK N° **14**

When they see an intruder, these birds make harsh 'kree-kree-kree' calls, then fly off to attack the unwanted visitor, giving a faster, angrier version of the call.

TRACK N° **15**

In this track, pairs are heard calling during the heat of the day from nests on the ledges of buildings. They give surprised-sounding 'aa-woo-woooo' calls.

16 | Red-eyed Dove
Tetere Jichojekundu

These doves are common residents, usually found in woodlands, along forest edges and in gardens. They occur mostly in pairs, but sometimes in small flocks.

Red-eyed doves eat seeds and fruits.

They build a substantial nest of twigs with a grass lining, deep in a bush or tree, in which 1–2 white eggs are laid.

17 | Ring-necked Dove
Tetere Mdogo

Ring-necked Doves are common, particularly at lower altitudes in bush country, but are absent from forests and very arid areas.

These doves are mostly seed eaters, but will also take insects if these are available.

The female makes a small nest in a tree, using twigs brought to her by the male. Occasionally, Ring-necked Doves have been known to use other birds' nests. They lay 1–2 white eggs.

TRACK N° **16**

In this track, we first hear the familiar territorial call given in the early morning; it is often translated as 'I am a Red-eyed Dove' or 'Who stole the Christmas tree?' Next we hear calls given by a courting pair.

TRACK N° **17**

This bird seems to say its name, or its call may be rendered as 'work harder'; in this track you will hear 2 different male doves giving this song. Later, you'll hear a pair giving various contented growling calls as they preen each other.

18 | Emerald-spotted Wood Dove
Pugi Kituku

 Emerald-spotted Wood Doves are small birds and are easily missed, as they spend most of their time foraging on the ground in dense vegetation. Their emerald spots are only seen in good light conditions.

 These doves eat mainly seeds, but occasionally also eat insects such as termites.

 The nest is a simple platform of sticks in a small tree or bush. They lay 1–2 creamish-white eggs.

19 | Great Blue Turaco
Shorobo–Mkuu

 These are large, spectacular and conspicuous birds. Mainly blue in colour, these turacos have a long tail and large, black crest, and occur in pairs or small family groups in forest canopies and wooded farmland in the west of the region. They often fan their tails. Their flight is poor, but they run nimbly along branches.

 Like most members of this family, Great Blue Turacos eat mainly the leaves, fruits and flower buds of various trees, but will even take algae from forest pools.

 They build a nest of sticks, with a shallow rim, in the dense foliage of a tall tree. They lay 1–3 white or pale glaucous-green eggs.

TRACK N° **19**

While they may call at any time of day, these birds are most vocal in the evening, before they roost. They travel in small groups; in this track a lead bird gives barks and purrs, which invite the entire group to respond with descending loud calls that reverberate through the forest. These calls help family members to form a cohesive unit.

TRACK N° **18**

This bird may call at any time of day. In this track, 2 birds call back and forth; they are undoubtedly neighbouring males, as the female does not share this call.

20 | Hartlaub's Turaco
Shorobo Buluu

These turacos are endemic to East Africa, occurring in pairs, mainly in highland forests, but also in gardens. They are usually seen as they swoop from tree to tree, flashing the bright red patches on their wings. They are common in the forests and large gardens around Nairobi.

 They eat mainly fruits, such as *Carissa spinarum* (edulis) and especially figs, but also caterpillars and beetles.

 The nest is a shallow platform of twigs. Very often 1–2 dull white eggs can be seen through the nest from below.

Virtually confined to Kenya, this is a very familiar bird in Nairobi's wooded suburbs. In this track, males are heard calling from their territory in the early morning; not far away, other males are doing the same.

21 | White-bellied Go-away-bird
Shorobo Tumbojeupe

White-bellied Go-away-birds are large grey-and-white birds, with a distinctive crest. They live in pairs or small family parties in semi-arid bush country, where they can be quite common.

 Their diet consists largely of the flowers and fruits of acacia and fig trees.

 An untidy nest of twigs is built high in an acacia tree, into which 1–4 glossy pale blue eggs are laid.

The 'waah' call is a very familiar sound in acacia bushland. It may lead into the full call, which is a descending series of 'kwaks', as it does in this track.

22 | White-browed Coucal
Dudumizi

 These coucals are common in thick vegetation, often near to water. Because of their distinctive call (see below), they are often called 'water bottle birds'. They are often seen flying away with a heavy flopping flight, before dropping into cover.

 White-browed Coucals have a varied diet of grasshoppers, locusts, ants, lizards, snakes, frogs and the eggs and chicks of other bird species.

 The nest is a large, untidy dome made of grass and twigs, lined with leaves and built among thick reeds or dense vegetation. These coucals lay 3–5 white eggs.

TRACK N° 22
They are silent for much of the year, but when ready to breed, pairs call to each other from a prominent perch, with a musical call that sounds like water running from a bottle. When they are disturbed, they fly off giving very harsh notes of disapproval.

23 | Red-chested Cuckoo
Kekeo Kifuachekundu

 Although they are common residents in woodlands and treed gardens and have a distinctive loud call, Red-chested Cuckoos can be very difficult to see. They usually occur singly and are very shy.

 They eat mainly caterpillars and insects.

 Unlike the eggs of the Dideric Cuckoo, the eggs of this cuckoo do not match those of the host. As many as 17 hosts have been recorded, the most common being Cape and Rüppell's robin-chats. As with most cuckoos, the Red-chested Cuckoo will remove one of its host's eggs, replacing it with her own and, on hatching, the young cuckoo will evict any unhatched eggs or newly hatched chicks from the nest.

TRACK N° 23
These birds chase each other through the woodlands, giving rapid 'titititi...' calls, then they settle down, and the male gives his well-known 'bring more rain' call. This excites the female, and the aerial display chase resumes.

24 | Dideric Cuckoo
Kekeo-Mdiriri

The female is duller than the male (above left).

Dideric Cuckoos are common residents in bush country below 2,000m. They usually call from treetops or exposed branches, which makes them a little easier to see than other cuckoos.

As is typical of cuckoos, their diet consists mainly of hairy caterpillars. Most other birds avoid these caterpillars, but this diet appears to have no ill effect on cuckoos.

Dideric Cuckoos are brood parasites. Like other cuckoos, they do not build nests, but instead lay their eggs in other bird's nests – in this case those of weavers. As many as 24 host species have been recorded and, in a single season, a female Dideric Cuckoo may lay as many as 26 eggs. Interestingly, the female always lays her eggs in the nest of the same species that reared her. Her eggs are very similar in colour to those of her host. Before laying an egg in the host nest, she removes the host's eggs and/or young. Soon after hatching, the young cuckoo often pushes any remaining unhatched eggs or chicks out of the nest.

TRACK N° 24

The call is a high-pitched, plaintive 'dee-dee-deediric' – hence this bird's common name. Males call to attract females and to advise rival males that the territory is occupied.

25 | Pearl-spotted Owlet
Kitaumande Madoa

Pearl-spotted Owlets, as their name suggests, are small (19cm) owls and are common residents in the dry bush country, preferring areas with acacias. They are frequently heard and seen during the daylight hours, when small birds often mob them, betraying their presence. They have an unusual feature: on the back of the head there are 2 dark marks that appear to be false eyes.

 Their diet consists mostly of insects, but, occasionally, they also prey on small rodents, small snakes and even small birds.

 They are unable to make their own nest holes, so they nest in a hole in a tree or take over an old nest built by a barbet or woodpecker. They lay 2–4 white eggs.

TRACK N° 25

Various calls are heard in this track, starting with a long sequence that reaches a climax, followed by a series of descending notes. Other birds may try to mob the owls and in the next part of the call you can hear aggressive calls in response to such intruders; at the end of the recording there's the sound of 2 Fan-tailed Ravens calling as the owls see them off.

26 | Montane Nightjar
Mbarawaji–Mlima

These birds are more often heard than seen. They are common in the highlands, along forest edges and in well-wooded urban areas. Nightjars feed at night over open ground and spend the day on the ground under a bush or tree, where their plumage makes them extremely difficult to see. During the day, they will only fly if disturbed, and then only for a short distance. Unfortunately, nightjars are very difficult to identify, but the combination of distinctive calls and subtle plumage differences are of help.

 They feed at night on airborne insects, beetles, grasshoppers and moths.

 Two eggs are laid on bare ground, usually under a bush or in the shade of a tree.

TRACK N° 26

In flight these nightjars give a rattling chatter, then land on a branch or roof and give a high-pitched, wavering whistle, which is a familiar nighttime sound.

27 | Slender-tailed Nightjar
Mbarawaji Mkiamwembamba

These are common nightjars that occur in dry acacia country, coastal scrub and grassland, often near water. They are more often seen than the previous species, as they forage low over the ground at dusk, sometimes in small congregations. During the day they roost on the ground, in long grass or among rocks.

Slender-tailed Nightjars feed mainly on airborne insects.

They lay 2 creamish-white eggs, with brown blotches, on bare ground near to a rock or small bush.

TRACK N° 27

Although not garden birds, these nightjars are often present around lodges in drier areas. When they first become active in the evening they give a bubbling call, then land on the ground to give their song, which sounds like a generator starting up.

28 | Little Swift
Teleka–Mdogo

These are small, black swifts with a conspicuous white rump and throat, usually seen flying around their nesting sites in cities, towns and under bridges. In the mornings and evenings, flocks wheel in noisy, tight display flight.

Little Swifts eat small, airborne insects. When feeding young, they gather a ball of small insects, which are mixed with saliva in the throat. When the chicks are small, the insect ball is broken up into small pieces, but when older they are fed the entire ball. A saliva ball may contain over 1,000 items!

These swifts breed colonially, building an untidy nest made of feathers and grass gathered in flight and glued together with saliva. They lay 1–3 white eggs.

TRACK N° 28

The trilling screams as these birds leave their roost in the mornings are a common noise in urban areas. When they return to feed their nestlings, they keep up a continuous higher-pitched twitter.

29 | Speckled Mousebird
Pasa-Mchirizi

Mousebirds are very acrobatic and prefer to hang rather than perch

Speckled Mousebirds are indigenous to Africa. Their common name derives from their habit of scampering along branches. These birds appear to have fur, rather than feathers, on the front of their bodies. This is because their feathers do not have barbules to keep the feather vanes together. This is probably the reason why they do not bathe in water but dust-bathe instead. Mousebirds rarely perch but instead hang onto branches. They roost at night in tight clusters, huddled closely together while hanging from a branch.

Mousebirds feed on a wide range of plants, leaves, flowers and buds, and ripe and unripe fruits, which makes them very unpopular with fruit growers.

These birds are co-operative breeders: the young from the previous brood help to rear and feed the young from the next brood. The nest is cup-shaped, built mostly of plant matter and lined with finer material. The female lays 1–5 creamish-white eggs.

TRACK N° **29**

Speckled Mousebirds give mostly harsh calls, but these are not aggressive; they are simply to maintain communication between group members.

30 | Lilac-breasted Roller
Chole

Perhaps the best known and most colourful birds seen on safari. These rollers prefer woodlands and open bush country, where there are trees to use as vantage points. Interestingly, in areas such as the Masai Mara National Reserve and the Serengeti National Park they can sometimes be seen using zebra and wildebeest as vantage points. They get their name from their distinctive aerial rolling displays.

 Rollers swoop down from their lookout posts onto prey such as beetles, grasshoppers and locusts. They also eat frogs, lizards, snakes and small rodents.

 They nest in decaying cavities in branches or, more rarely, in termite mounds, and lay 2–3 smooth white eggs.

TRACK N° **30**

In this track a male sitting on a tree barks out his harsh call and then takes to the air. From a height he enters a tumbling display with his wings rocking backwards and forwards, flashing brilliant colours, while giving harsh 'kak' notes to impress a female on a neighbouring tree.

31 | Woodland Kingfisher
Kichi Buluu

These distinctive blue and white kingfishers, with their striking, large, red and black bills, are common in woodlands, grassland and on forest edges, not necessarily near to water, and mainly below 1,500m. They are usually seen perching conspicuously on natural or man-made vantage points.

 Woodland Kingfishers are carnivorous, feeding on a mixed diet of insects, lizards, frogs, scorpions and butterflies. In spite of the name 'kingfisher', fish do not form an important part of this species' diet.

 They lay 2–3 white eggs in a natural tree hole or in a nest hole abandoned by a barbet or woodpecker.

TRACK N° **31**

During the day birds call to each other with a rapid-fire 'chit-chit-chit', but in the early morning they welcome the day with a musical descending rattle; they give the same call before going to roost in the evening.

A female bird hovers before diving for its fish prey.

32 | Pied Kingfisher
Kichi Mtilili

These kingfishers are common residents at inland waters and on the coast. They are particularly common in Uganda, where an average 16 birds per kilometre were counted along the Kazinga Channel. The sexes are easily distinguished; the male has 2 bands across its chest, while the female has a single broken band.

 Pied Kingfishers eat mostly fish; they hover over the water until they spot a fish, and then plunge dive into the water, piercing the prey with the tip of their long, straight, sharp bill. The fish is then taken to a perch where it is beaten before being swallowed. Occasionally, they will also eat dragonflies, water beetles and other small insects.

 The nest is an oval chamber located at the end of a long tunnel (sometimes over a metre long), excavated in a river bank. The female lays 1–5 glossy white eggs. The birds nest colonially in western lakes; they are co-operative breeders, so the progeny from the previous year assist in raising their parents' latest brood.

TRACK N° **32**

Theirs is not a very musical call, but they communicate constantly with high, chittering calls, given in flight and while perched.

An immature Little Bee-eater

33 | Little Bee-eater
Kinega Mdogo

Little Bee-eaters occur in pairs or in family groups and are common in bush country, open woodlands and in reeds at the edges of rivers and marshes. They are often confused with the larger, darker and more richly coloured Cinnamon-chested Bee-eaters, which are birds of the highland forests.

 They eat flying bees, dragonflies, butterflies and other insects, and hunt their prey by swooping from a branch and catching it with a loud snap. Often they return to the same branch or to one nearby, where they beat the prey to soften it before they eat.

 Their nest is a burrow, built by both sexes, usually in the side of a river bank. At the end of the burrow is an unlined nest chamber into which the female lays 4–6 translucent pinkish eggs, which later turn chalky white.

TRACK N° **33**

For most of the year these familiar birds of the open country give single calls, but when nesting season arrives, they give lively, strident, chittering calls – their equivalent of a song. These calls are often associated with courtship feeding, during which males present females with tasty insect treats.

A bee-eater with an insect treat

34 | Northern Carmine Bee-eater
Kinega Mwekundu

Attractive and unmistakable, these are brilliant carmine-red bee-eaters, with contrasting darker heads. They may occur singly or in flocks, visiting northern and northeastern Kenya, as well as northeastern Tanzania, from September to April, although a few occasionally nest near Lake Turkana. At times they are very common along the coast, with some non-breeders staying on all year.

 They feed on various insects, grasshoppers, locusts and bees. Interestingly, these bee-eaters are able to discharge the venom from a bee without having to land and rub it against a branch, as other bee-eaters have to do. They have occasionally been seen sitting on the backs of zebra and Kori Bustards, using them as unwitting beaters to flush insects, and then swooping down to catch any items of prey that have been disturbed.

 This bee-eater breeds in large, conspicuous colonies in river banks and on level ground (at Ileret near Lake Turkana). Both sexes dig a burrow into which the female lays 2–5 glossy white eggs. Occasionally, helpers will assist with feeding the young.

TRACK N° **34**

When displaying, these birds give fairly harsh but musical calls. A disturbed bird, however, gives very harsh calls expressing its discontent before flying off.

35 | European Bee-eater
Kinega–Ulaya

 These bee-eaters are common migrants, which are mostly heard and seen high in the sky, just ahead of storm clouds. Most are seen passing through the region from September to October, on their way further south, or on their return journey, from March to May. At night, they roost in tall eucalyptus trees.

 They feed on a variety of insects, which are caught and eaten on the wing.

 European Bee-eaters do not nest in our region: in Europe they breed in colonies, digging nest tunnels into sandbanks.

TRACK N° **35**

Birders always look forward to the return of these bee-eaters from Europe in September. The first flocks make soft purring calls as they feed overhead. At their roost, they are much noisier, with all individuals calling at the same time.

36 | African Hoopoe
Hudihudi (Ndututu)–Africa

 These are common, distinctive residents found in a wide range of habitats. The long, decurved bill and crest are characteristic. African Hoopoes are usually seen walking on the ground, looking for food. When disturbed or alarmed, they raise their crest like a fan.

 They forage on the ground probing for beetle larvae and ant lions, ants, spiders and small lizards.

 The nest is always in a cavity, an old woodpecker nest hole or a termite mound. They do not excavate their own holes. The nest cavity is sparsely lined with dry grass, and the female lays 4–9 white, buff or pale blue, finely blotched eggs.

TRACK N° **36**

This is another familiar call in woodlands and gardens. African Hoopoes call even during the hottest part of the day.

37 | Green Wood-Hoopoe
Gegemela Domojekundu

Green Wood-Hoopoes are common residents in forests and woodlands, especially acacia woodlands. They occur in noisy family parties, and are usually seen flying from tree to tree and climbing over tree trunks and branches, exploring cracks for food. Family parties defend their territories. Green Wood-Hoopoes have an unusual feature: their preen gland produces an unpleasant scent that is used to deter potential predators.

 They eat mainly insects and grubs, which they find under bark.

 Green Wood-Hoopoes nest in natural cavities or in old woodpecker holes, laying 2–5 pale greenish-blue eggs. They are co-operative breeders; helpers continue to feed the young long after they have left the nest.

TRACK N° 37

The lead male gives a few notes inviting the other members of his group to join in: together they give a bowing display that includes slowly raising and lowering their tails.

38 | Silvery-cheeked Hornbill
Hondohondo kijivu

These very large black and white birds are usually found in pairs or family parties in highland forests and woodlands, from sea level to 2,600m. They often leave their forest habitat and visit towns and cities, such as Nairobi, in search of fruiting trees. When flying, their wing beats make a loud, clear whooshing sound.

 They feed mostly on fruits, such as figs, but also eat small nuts, bird eggs and nestlings.

 The nest is usually a natural hole in a tree. Once inside, the female seals the entrance, leaving a narrow slit through which she is fed. She lays 1–2 white eggs, but usually only a single chick is fledged. She stays in the nest until the chick is ready to fledge, about 77–80 days after laying, then she breaks out.

TRACK N° 38

Birds call from high up in evergreen trees. They are especially noisy in the early mornings and in evenings, calling in flight as they fly off to their roosts.

The female has a maroon-tipped bill.

39 | African Grey Hornbill
Hondohondo

These hornbills are common residents that usually occur in pairs, or small family parties, in woodlands and wooded grasslands. They are often seen as they fly from tree to tree with a hornbill's characteristic heavy, undulating flight. Displaying birds point their bill skywards, rock back and forth and flick their wings.

 They eat fruits, insects such as grasshoppers and beetles, tree frogs, chameleons and, occasionally, rodents, which they snatch from the ground.

 They nest in a natural tree hole. The female enters the nest and seals its entrance, leaving only a narrow slit through which her mate feeds her. After about a week, she lays 3–5 white eggs at 1–7-day intervals. Incubation begins as the first egg is laid, so chicks hatch at roughly the same time intervals at which the eggs were laid. The female breaks out of the nest when the oldest chick is about 25 days old and reseals the entrance. The chicks eventually break out at intervals; the younger chicks reseal the entrance until they are ready to leave.

TRACK N° **39**

For such small hornbills theirs is quite a complex call, and it is a well-known sound of dry bushland areas. Birds call from a high perch on top of a tree, and pairs communicate over long distances.

40 | Yellow-rumped Tinkerbird
Tingitingi Kiunonjano

Yellow-rumped Tinkerbirds are common residents in highland forests, woodlands and gardens. They are more often heard than seen, as they forage through bushes, treetops and tangled vines.

 Tinkerbirds eat fruits and favour figs and various berries, but they also feed on insects.

 They excavate their own nest hole, usually in a dead tree or under a dead branch. The entrance hole is circular, just wide enough for the bird to enter. The female lays 2–3 white eggs.

TRACK N° **40**

For most of the year, the male defends his territory, calling throughout the day. The call, given for long periods, is a series of 5–7 hollow 'tink' notes with pauses between sets.

41 | Lesser Honeyguide
Kiongozi Mdogo

These are common, solitary and inconspicuous birds that are often overlooked, as they are only conspicuous in flight, when their white outer tail feathers are seen. They often sit quietly in trees and occur in a variety of habitats, including forests, woodlands, bush country and cultivated areas.

 Lesser Honeyguides feed mainly on bees, beeswax and insects. In fact, honeyguides are the only birds in the world that can digest beeswax.

 They are brood parasites, laying their eggs in the nest of a hole-nesting bird, usually a barbet. Newly hatched honeyguides have a sharp bill with hooks, used to kill all the host chicks.

TRACK N° **41**

In the breeding season the male calls at any time of day, giving a 'chew..., pwip, pwip pwip pwip pwip' from a regular perch. When he finds a nesting barbet he gives a special chittering call to attract a mate to this potential host nest, although the barbets always try to chase Lesser Honeyguides away.

The juvenile has yellowish underparts.

42 | Greater Honeyguide
Kiongozi Mkubwa

The Greater Honeyguide's Latin name is *Indicator indicator*, a reference to its habit of leading humans and mammals, such as honey badgers, to beehives, in the hope that these assistants will open the nest for the honey, and that they will be rewarded with the beeswax, which forms their main diet.

 In addition to beeswax, Greater Honeyguides also occasionally feed on bees, their eggs and their larvae. A 16th-century Dominican missionary in Mozambique first observed their unusual feeding habits. He noticed that honeyguides were eating wax from the altar candles!

 Like all honeyguides, Greater Honeyguides are brood parasites that lay their eggs in the nests of hole-nesting birds. Their hosts range from bee-eaters to swallows, barbets and woodpeckers. Young birds are fed insects by their foster parents.

TRACK N° **42**

Males defend their territories all year, giving a distinctive call from regular song posts. As they guide a honey-hunting assistant to the nest, they give a special barking chatter that changes to rapid chattering the closer they get.

43 | Nubian Woodpecker
Kigong'ota-Mnubi

 Nubian Woodpeckers are common residents of open bush and acacia woodlands. Members of a pair forage independently, remaining in vocal contact with each other by duetting. They also drum on trees during courtship displays and to proclaim their territory.

 They feed mostly in trees, tapping dead branches in search of insects, spiders and various larvae, and using their long tongues to reach under loose bark. Occasionally they drop to the ground to eat ants and beetles.

 Nubian Woodpeckers excavate a nest hole in a tree or, occasionally, in a fence post or an earth bank and lay 2–5 white eggs.

44 | Cardinal Woodpecker
Kigong'ota Kiparachekundu

 These are small, common and widespread woodpeckers, usually occurring in pairs along forest edges, in open woodlands or in dry bush country. They call to each other frequently to maintain contact. When excited they often raise a short crest.

 They probe tree trunks, branches, twigs, bushes of all sizes and vines to glean beetle and moth larvae and termites, and will occasionally eat fruits.

 The nest hole is normally situated on the underside of a branch and may contain 2–3 white eggs.

TRACK N° **43**

The most widespread large woodpeckers, and among the most vocal. Their call is a loud, far-carrying 'ching, ching, ching'. A bird will start calling, then its mate will join in and duet with it from another tree.

TRACK N° **44**

These small common woodpeckers give rasping 'krrrik-krrrik-krrrik-krrrik-krrrik' calls in display or alarm, either from a perch or in flight.

45 | Chinspot Batis
Tatata Kidoacheusi

These batises are common and widespread, tame residents that are found in a wide variety of habitats, including bush country, acacia woodlands and forest edges.

They forage in the tree canopy for insects, caterpillars and spiders.

They build small cup nests made of fine grass and fibres, strengthened with spider's web and camouflaged with layers of lichen. These nests blend into the tree, making them difficult to see. They are lined with fine grass and the female lays 1–3 pale grey-green or green-blue eggs.

TRACK N° **45**

This well-known song is a 2-toned 'pi-poo'. When the female arrives, the male flies excitedly around her, clicking his wings and making strange burry purrs and clicks.

46 | White-crested Helmetshrike
Mlali Mweupe

Helmetshrikes are highly sociable birds, always occurring in flocks of 6–30 individuals that stay in noisy contact with one another. Their flight is graceful and almost butterfly-like. These birds are common residents in acacia and bush country.

They feed on caterpillars, beetles, grasshoppers, mantises and termites.

Co-operative breeders, all members of the group build the nest and help to incubate, brood and feed the young. The nest is a smooth, compact cup made of small pieces of bark, bound with spider's web and lined with small bits of bark, grass and lichen. The female lays 3–5 pale pink or buff eggs, with purple, brown and grey blotches and spots.

TRACK N° **46**

As these birds move through the woodlands they remain in contact using chittering calls and bill snaps. Now and again group members gather and call together before they fly off to another area, looking a bit like large black and white butterflies.

47 | Grey-headed Bushshrike
Kuwekuwe Kichwakijivu

These are large, bulky birds that have a massive bill and bright yellow eyes. They occur in pairs in acacia woodlands and riverine forests, and prefer dense vegetation. Except when calling, they are surprisingly easy to overlook, as they are skulking and elusive, usually foraging in the canopy.

 They eat a large variety of food including grasshoppers, mantises, bees, termites, chameleons, small snakes, rodents, bats and birds, eggs and chicks.

 The nest is an untidy bowl made of twigs lined with dry leaves, soft grass and fibrous roots. The female lays 2–4 glossy pinkish-white eggs with chestnut and purplish-brown blotches.

48 | Sulphur-breasted (Orange-breasted) Bushshrike
Kuwekuwe Manjano

Striking and common, Orange-breasted Bushshrikes are nevertheless easily overlooked, as they keep to dense vegetation in woodlands and savanna.

 They consume small insects, wasps, caterpillars, mantises, beetles and grubs.

 The nest is a flimsy platform made of grass and fine dry twigs, lined with rootlets and creeper tendrils. The female lays 1–3 greenish-white eggs, heavily streaked, blotched and spotted in various shades of brown.

TRACK N° **47**

The male gives a loud musical piping. In flight from one perch to another he gives an angry-sounding, descending 'wehh–wehh–wehh–wehh–wehh–wehh', but on landing pipes out a mournful series of ventriloquial notes, the last of which rises. When excited, he snaps his bill and gives strange wails.

TRACK N° **48**

A distinctive dry woodlands call, with a series of ringing double, then single, identical notes.

49 | Brown-crowned Tchagra
Kikuche Kichwachekundu

50 | Black-crowned Tchagra
Kikuche Kichwacheusi

 Brown-crowned Tchagras are shy and skulking birds found in a variety of wooded and dry habitats. They prefer dense thickets. All tchagras have a characteristic display flight.

 These tchagras run and hop about, feeding on or near the ground, often beneath bushes. They eat mainly insects such as grasshoppers, caterpillars and beetles.

 Their nest is a shallow-walled cup made of rootlets, fine twigs and coarse grass, lined with fine grass and feathers. They lay 2–4 whitish eggs with small dark brown spots and blotches.

 These locally common tchagras are also shy, skulking birds found in a variety of open wooded habitats, in bushy grassland and in dry country.

 They feed on or near the ground, or low down in bushes and shrubs, taking mainly grasshoppers, termites and beetles, but also small frogs and lizards.

 A compact, shallow cup nest is built out of rootlets and fine twigs, lined with finer rootlets and grass. The female lays 2–3 white eggs, with reddish-purple and brown spots and blotches.

TRACK N° 49

In courtship display these birds shoot up into the air and, while 'parachuting' down, give a distinctive, cheerful set of descending notes. When hidden in the bush they give various harsh calls.

TRACK N° 50

Their lazy, fluty, rising and falling whistled call is common in some open scrubby areas; excited, harsher calls are usually given from hidden birds – in this track they are probably those of a female responding to a male's song.

51 | Black-backed Puffback
Chukui Kiunocheupe

Common birds, usually found in pairs along forest edges, in woodlands and gardens, Black-backed Puffbacks spend most of their time in the canopy. They often draw attention to themselves by their unusual contact calls. The displaying males erect their rump feathers into a puffy white ball, hence the common name 'puffback'.

 They feed on beetles, caterpillars, some fruits and the buds of acacia trees.

 The nest is a small, deep cup of grass, roots and bark strips, bound together with spider's web and sometimes decorated with pieces of lichen. The female lays 2–4 white or pale cream eggs with brown spots and streaks.

52 | Slate-coloured Boubou
Tiva Kijivucheusi

Slate-coloured Boubous are widespread residents, usually found below 2,200m in thickets in dry bush country, but they also occur in coastal scrub and woodlands. They are shy birds, often skulking on the ground, always within thick cover.

 They eat grasshoppers, termites, bees, wasps and small butterflies.

 These boubous build a loose, open cup nest out of bark fibre, fine rootlets and twiglets, in which the female lays 2–3 pale blue eggs with fine red-brown speckling.

TRACK N° **51**

The male chatters loudly in the bush, giving a variety of noises and building up to a display flight in which his back feathers are raised like a snowball; he then flies into the open with clicking wings and gives a sequence of identical whiplash notes.

TRACK N° **52**

Boubous have remarkably varied repertoires. Members of a pair will duet, the female uttering harsh notes, and the male singing musical ones. Their different phrases are timed so perfectly that it is like listening to a single bird.

53 | Tropical Boubou
Tiva Rangimbili

Pairs of Tropical Boubous occur in upland forests, woodlands, riverine thickets, coastal scrub and gardens. They forage low down and, occasionally, in leaf itter. Though shy, they draw attention with their characteristic, clear, bell-like whistles, which have earned them the nickname 'bell birds'.

They feed on mantises, termites, beetles, caterpillars and, occasionally, on chameleons, skinks, small rodents, bird eggs and nestlings.

The nest is an open, shallow bowl, made of fine twigs and rootlets, bound with spider webs and sparsely lined with fine rootlets. The female lays 2–3 pale blue to green-blue eggs, flecked with brown.

TRACK N° 53

This boubou also has a varied repertoire. Known as the bell bird of East Africa, it gives many ringing tones, some sounding like hinges in need of oiling and interspersed with harsh, clacking noises.

54 | Black-headed Gonolek
Tiva Kichwacheusi

These are skulking, beautiful and unmistakable birds that occur west of the Great Rift Valley in bush country, often near to water, in thick vegetation or in neglected areas of cultivation. They are common around Lake Victoria.

Their food consists of insects, caterpillars and small fruits.

The nest is an open, loosely constructed cup, made of rootlets, grass and bark fibres, and lined with fine rootlets. The 2 pale blue or bluish-green eggs have heavy reddish-brown and grey blotching.

TRACK N° 54

Despite its name, this is another species of boubou. It mixes musical ringing calls with harsh, ratchety sounds.

55 | Brubru
Kuwekuwe Mbavunyekundu

Common residents, Brubrus are small birds of bush country and woodlands, but favour acacia woodlands. They are active birds, usually seen searching canopy foliage for insects. They could easily be overlooked were it not for their characteristic song.

 Insects, including caterpillars, ants, beetles and spiders, make up their diet.

 They build an attractive, small, open cup nest using small, fine twigs, tendrils and pieces of bark, held together with spider's web. The outside of the nest is covered in lichen, which camouflages it against the tree branches.

56 | Grey-backed Fiscal
Mbwigu Kijivu

Locally common in woodlands and acacia country, Grey-backed Fiscals frequently occur near water. They are usually found in small, conspicuous, sociable parties, often displaying noisily on branches, waving their tails and fluttering their wings.

 They feed on driver ants, moths, small frogs, toads and nestlings.

 The nest is a compact, untidy, open cup, built of twigs and rootlets, and lined with fine grass and small feathers. The female lays 2–4 pale yellowish eggs with a few brown and grey spots.

TRACK N° 55

The male's call, which is reminiscent of a ringing alarm, is associated with dry bush country. The female answers with a harsh 'nyehh'. The pair then join in a duet, the female responding to the male's call with 'chu chu' notes.

TRACK N° 56

In this track several birds sing together as a family unit, sitting close together, with their long tails waving furiously, then a single bird gives a harsh, frog-like alarm call, and is later joined by other members.

57 | Northern (Common) Fiscal
Mbwigu Mgongomweupe

Northern Fiscals are common residents, particularly in the highlands. They occur even in towns and villages, perched singly or in pairs on telephone poles and wires.

They swoop down from elevated perches to snatch insects like crickets, grasshoppers, mantises, locusts and termites. Larger prey items like rodents, frogs, snakes, skinks and young birds are often impaled on thorns or barbed wire, or wedged into a cleft in a branch, hence the nickname 'butcher birds'; the scientific name *lanius* means 'butcher'.

The nest is a deep, bulky cup of twigs, leaves, bark fibres and grass in which 1–6 cream or pale green eggs with brown and grey spots are laid.

TRACK N° 57

Sitting on a prominent perch the male utters a few harsh notes that precede a mournful 'pccccceeee, peeeeeeee' whistle, given 2 or 3 times.

58 | Black-headed Oriole
Naiwa (Kubwiro) Mweusi

These common residents occur along forest edges, in woodlands and in gardens, where they spend most of their time in the treetops. They are highly vocal, particularly early in the morning.

They forage for fruits and insects inside the canopy and are usually seen flying from tree to tree.

A shallow cup nest is suspended between 2–3 horizontal branches, and is constructed from fine fibres, moss, grass and spider's web. Inside, the nest is thinly lined with fine grass and rootlets. The female lays 1–3 white or creamish-buff eggs, with red-brown blotches and spots.

TRACK N° 58

A frequent visitor to gardens, this bird gives loud, cheerful, ringing calls; it almost seems to be saying 'I'm an oriole'.

59 | Fork-tailed Drongo
Mlamba Mikiapanda

Common residents in woodlands, along forest edges and in acacia and thornbush country, these birds perch prominently on exposed branches and hunt both in the air and on the ground. Aggressive at times, Fork-tailed Drongos mob birds of prey, even large eagles such as Bateleurs.

Drongos feed mostly on insects such as grasshoppers, beetles, winged termites, bees, butterflies and cicadas, but also occasionally take small birds. They sometimes use game such as zebra as hunting perches.

The nest is a shallow cup made of rootlets, plant stems and creeper tendrils, bound and camouflaged with spider's web. The female lays 2–3 white, cream or pinkish eggs with freckles and small reddish-brown blotches.

TRACK N° **59**

A widespread bird of the bush
that gives a long series of harsh, skirling churrs.

60 | Pied Crow
Kunguru Mweupe

Pied Crows are common residents, and occur in large flocks near human habitation. Their flight is distinctive and laboured, with slow wing beats; they often soar to considerable heights.

Omnivorous, they forage for carrion, vegetable matter and insects, visit refuse dumps, scavenge from carcasses, raid heronries for nestlings and chicks and, occasionally, glean parasites from domestic and game mammals.

The nest is a bulky structure of sticks, twigs and roots and may include bits of wire. The deep cup is lined with grass, mud, wool – even string! It is usually at the top of a tall tree but may also be situated on a telephone pole, pylon or radio mast. The 1–7 pale, glossy, greenish or blue-green eggs have grey-brown spots.

TRACK N° **60**

Like most crows this bird caws,
but these caws vary considerably.

61 | African Paradise Flycatcher
Chechele Mwekundu

A male sitting on the nest (above left); a female perched (above right)

 African Paradise Flycatchers are common and usually occur in pairs in forests, woodlands, acacia country and gardens. They are easily overlooked unless heard or seen flying. Two distinct colour forms occur; a white form, which has a white back and tail and white in the wings; and a rufous form, which has an orange-rufous back and tail. These flycatchers forage among leaves and are always on the move, occasionally dashing from one tree to another, with a distinct, graceful, undulating flight.

 They catch insects in flight, including grasshoppers, cicadas, moths, butterflies, flying ants, termites and spiders.

 A small, neat, shallow nest cup is built out of vegetable fibres, little pieces of bark, dried leaves, rootlets and tendrils, all bound together and covered with spider's web and decorated with lichen. It is lined with fine rootlets and dry grass. The female lays 1–5 creamish or pink eggs, with sparse reddish-brown spots. The fast-growing chicks soon find the nest too small. Red-chested Cuckoos often parasitise African Paradise Flycatcher nests.

TRACK N° 61

The song is preceded by a chattering of metallic mixed notes, climaxing in a series of similar but louder notes.

62 | White-bellied Tit
Chambombe Tumbojeupe

These tits occur in pairs or family parties. Very active and vocal, they are always on the move, foraging in trees, and are common in a variety of habitats, including forest edges and gardens.

White-bellied Tits forage just under the tree canopy and on tree trunks for spiders and various insects.

The nest is a soft pad of bark fibres, hair, fur and lichen, usually situated in a hole in a tree trunk or at the end of a broken branch. The female lays 3–5 eggs with sparse maroon specks.

63 | Rufous-naped Lark
Kipozamataza Kisogochekundu

These, the most common larks, are resident in open plains and grassy bush country. Usually they are seen and heard as they sing from a termite mound or small bush. They rise from the ground with a jerky action, at which time their red wing patches are conspicuous.

They feed on beetles, grasshoppers and termites, but also eat spiders, earthworms and grass seeds.

A cup nest of dry grass, lined with rootlets and finer material, is located in a scrape on the ground, usually set against a tuft of grass or a shrub. The back and sides of the nest are built up to form a flimsy-looking dome. Females lay 2–4 dull white or pale cream eggs with grey-brown spots and blotches.

TRACK N° **62**

They mostly give the dry rasps typical of a tit, but these sometimes give way to musical chattering and sweeter notes.

TRACK N° **63**

Most of the time this species sings from a prominent perch. It repeats the same phrase for long periods, and then switches to another, similar phrase, which it then repeats for long periods.

64 | Common Bulbul
Sholwe (Shore)

Found in most habitats, including gardens, these are among the most common African birds. The head appears slightly crested at times, and the yellow undertail coverts are conspicuous.

Common Bulbuls eat a variety of wild and cultivated fruits, flowers, nectar, insects and, occasionally, seeds. They can be a nuisance at safari camps with open dining, as they steal food, especially sugar.

The nest is a thin, shallow bowl built of twigs and stems, often bound together with spider's web and lined with fine grasses and rootlets. The female normally lays 2 eggs, which vary in colour.

TRACK N° **64**

Common Bulbuls are not the greatest songsters, although their song has a cheerful tone.

65 | Yellow-whiskered Greenbul
Nyembelele Sharubunjano

These are common residents in forests, dense scrub and gardens. Although they are among the most ubiquitous forest birds, they are far more often heard than seen.

They are omnivorous, eating fruits and berries as well as spiders, grasshoppers, caterpillars, moths and winged termites.

Their nest is a loosely built cup, with an outer layer of twigs, rootlets and strips of bark. The inside of the nest comprises dried leaves bound together with spider's web and lined with fine rootlets and dry grass. It may contain 1–4 white or grey eggs, with brown or purple-brown markings.

TRACK N° **65**

This greenbul could win the prize for most monotonous singer! It sings from a concealed position almost throughout the day, giving a very long series of cheerful chips and chatters. If you approach too closely, it will give a strident series of identical 'chip' notes.

43

66 | Sombre Greenbul
Nyemelele jichojeupe

These are common coastal birds, but they also occur in the Kenyan highlands. Shy and skulking, they inhabit thick vegetation and are difficult to see, except when singing.

They forage in trees and bushes for insects, fruits and berries.

The nest is a thin, flimsy, shallow cup of twigs, rootlets, fibres and dry grass, lined with more fine grass and fibres. The female lays 1–3 eggs with red-brown spots and streaks.

TRACK N° 66

This greenbul is another cheerful singer. In the early morning it finds a prominent perch, such as a telephone wire, from which it sings, but for the rest of the day it remains concealed in vegetation and gives calls that are less sweet than the morning song.

67 | Lesser-striped Swallow
Mbayuwayu-Michirizi

Common residents, Lesser-striped Swallows occur in pairs or small groups throughout the region, except in forests. They are often associated with human habitation, building their nests on buildings and bridges. The distinctive forked tail can be opened and closed during flight, for manoeuvrability.

They feed on airborne insects, often near cattle and game animals, taking insects disturbed by their hooves.

The nest is retort-shaped – a bulb with a long entrance tunnel made of mud pellets – usually located under the eaves of a roof, veranda or bridge or under a large branch. The bowl is lined with grass and feathers and the female lays 2–4 glossy white eggs. The nests are often taken over by White-rumped Swifts and sparrows.

TRACK N° 67

These birds have amazing calls: they perch and give a strange descending series of nasal, tinny notes. In flight, they give a loud 'tiu tiu tiu'.

68 | Red-rumped Swallow
Mbayuwayu Kiunochekundu

Common and widespread in the region, especially above 1,000m, these birds generally inhabit rocky hills and dry country, but also occur in the lowlands around Lake Victoria.

 They feed on airborne insects.

 The nest is a bowl, made of mud pellets and dry grass stems, with a long entrance tunnel. It is lined with grass and feathers and is usually built in a cave, on a building or under a road culvert or bridge. The female lays 4–5 glossy white eggs with fine red-brown speckling.

TRACK N° 68

Perched birds sing a medley of soft chips punctuated by a loud snoring 'sweeech'. In flight they give a diagnostic and repetitive 'schwerp'.

69 | Lesser Swamp Warbler
Shoro Mdomomwembamba

Lesser Swamp Warblers are common residents found in most reed beds, where they draw attention to themselves with their characteristic calls. Although more often heard than seen, they appear briefly as they jump from reed to reed, low down in the vegetation. They may also sit on exposed perches for just a few brief moments.

 They forage in reed and papyrus beds at mid-level or just above the water, taking mostly insects but occasionally small frogs.

 The nest is a deep, conical cup made of dry reed stems and coarse grass, lined with strips of fine grass. The female lays 2–3 white or greenish-white eggs, with black or dark grey freckling.

TRACK N° 69

Even when this bird is hidden from sight, its sweet singing is wonderful to hear, less so the other calls it gives, such as contact calls – these harsh notes may be heard at any time of day, but are often given immediately before the song.

70 | Singing Cisticola
Kidenenda–Kiwimbo

Common but localised upland residents, Singing Cisticolas occur in pairs or family parties and are particularly numerous in Nairobi gardens. They inhabit dense vegetation and hedgerows. They are secretive, except when the male is calling from a perch.

They forage close to the ground for small beetles, caterpillars, moths and grasshoppers.

A flimsy, domed nest is built out of dry grass, fine grass seed heads and bark fibres, and lined with plant down. The nest is sewn onto 2–3 broad leaves using spider silk, often with a leaf positioned over the top. The female lays 2–4 white or creamish-pink eggs with red-brown freckling and spots. Pin-tailed Whydahs often parasitise these nests.

TRACK N° **70**

Both sexes call together as one bird, their 'a-choo' call sounding like a constant series of sneezes. They also give a call that sounds like 'rich kid'.

71 | Rattling Cisticola
Kidenenda–Taratara

Rattling Cisticolas are common and conspicuous residents of acacia country and cultivation, found in pairs or in family parties. They draw attention to themselves with their noisy scolding call, which is given from the tops of bushes.

They forage low down among grass and bushes, or on the ground for beetles, ants, termites and grasshoppers.

The nest is a broad oval or pear shape, with a side entrance, loosely built out of dry grass and bound together with spider's web. It is lined with finer grass, seed heads and plant down. The female lays 2–5 white or bright blue eggs, with red-brown spots and blotches.

TRACK N° **71**

There is nothing very musical in this bird's song, which comprises a few introductory notes followed by a rattle. Its regular call is a series of harsh, complaining notes.

72 | Tawny-flanked Prinia
Shoro Bawakahawia

These common and widespread residents occur in pairs or in small family groups. They frequent rank grass, as well as scrub along streams, forest edges and gardens, and also occur in overgrown cultivated areas. They have a distinctive jerky flight. Males call from an exposed perch, often cocking the tail over the back, swivelling and fanning it when excited.

 They forage low down within cover, gleaning insects.

 An oval-shaped, thin-walled nest with a narrow side-top entrance is made from fine green grass blades, closely woven and interlaced. The female lays 1–6 eggs that are highly variable in colour.

73 | Yellow-breasted Apalis
Kilokolo Kifuanjano

Yellow-breasted Apalises are resident birds that usually occur in pairs in a variety of habitats from forests and woodlands to bush. They favour acacias.

 These birds forage in the canopy for mantises, ants, caterpillars, spiders, fruits and nectar.

 The nest is a purse-shaped bag, domed or semi-domed, with a side-top entrance and is suspended from the end of a branch. It is made from lichens bound together with spider webs. The female lays 2–4 glossy, pale blue-green eggs with small, red-brown spots.

TRACK N° **72**

This species buzzes away in thick grassland and scrub, and then climbs a stem to give its rattling song.

TRACK N° **73**

The male's call sounds like a galloping horse; the female accompanies him by giving low growls.

74 | Grey-capped Warbler
Shoro Kichwakijivu

Large, shy warblers, they inhabit thick scrub, forest undergrowth and dense vegetation, often along streams and rivers, and also occur in suburban gardens. Often heard, they can be difficult to see.

 Insects such as mantises, caterpillars, small grasshoppers and spiders comprise their diet.

 They build a domed nest, with a side entrance that has a small platform and porch, using dry grass, fibres, tendrils, leaves and spider's web, all lined with rootlets and vegetable down. It hangs from a branch within the shade of thick vegetation. The female lays 2–3 glossy white, pink or pale blue eggs, which sometimes have purple markings.

TRACK N° **74**

A very sweet songster with a varied repertoire; like so many African birds, Grey-capped Warblers duet, the female giving different calls, but timed so that it sounds like just a single bird is singing.

75 | Grey-backed Camaroptera
Kibwirosagi

Common and widespread residents, Grey-backed Camaropteras skulk in thick undergrowth and bush and would be easy to overlook, were it not for their bleating alarm calls.

 They forage on the ground, or low down in dense thickets, for caterpillars, small mantises, termite larvae, spiders and other small insects.

 They build an unusual nest; 2 large leaves are sewn together with spider silk, forming a pocket with an opening on one side near the top. Another leaf is then pulled down and stitched to form a roof. The female lays 2–4 glossy white or pale blue eggs, sometimes with red-brown blotches.

TRACK N° **75**

These birds are sometimes known as 'Bleating Warblers' because they give a strange bleat. They also have a variety of different calls including nasal slurs and clicking calls, all of which are used frequently.

76 | Arrow-marked Babbler
Zogoyogo Bawa-Mishale

77 | Montane (Kikuyu) White-eye
Kinengenenge-Mlima

Locally common, Arrow-marked Babblers forage in family groups among thick, shrubby undergrowth and tall grass. Usually, one member of the group is seen in low flight as it moves to another bush, followed, in rapid succession, by the remaining members of the group. These groups defend their territory.

Babblers forage for insects, mainly grasshoppers, termites, caterpillars and beetles.

They are co-operative breeders: other adults will assist a pair in raising their young. They build a bulky, untidy nest of broad-bladed grass and large leaves. The nest bowl is lined with rootlets, fine fibres and dry grass. The female lays 2–5 bright blue eggs.

Common residents of highland forests and gardens, Montane White-eyes occur in small flocks, except when breeding. They love to bathe in rain or dew-soaked foliage.

They glean small insects from foliage, often hanging upside down to do so, but also feed on soft fruits and pierce the bases of flowers to drink nectar.

A straggly looking cup nest is built of moss, lichens and fine bark, all bound together with spider's web. The female lays 2–3 blue or white eggs.

TRACK N° 76

Babblers travel in family groups and have loud, usually harsh, calls. All the members of a group may line up on a branch, giving the same raucous call.

TRACK N° 77

Structurally and tonally the calls of white-eyes all sound very similar, usually comprising a downslurred 'seeu', although Montane White-eyes sound louder and sharper. Less frequently, they also sing sweet songs.

78 | Greater Blue-eared Starling
Kuzi Machanjano

Common and widespread residents, pairs or small flocks of Greater Blue-eared Starlings occur in a variety of habitats, including cities and towns.

They feed mainly on the ground, taking insects, seeds and fallen fruits, but also sometimes feed in the tops of fruiting trees.

The nest is a bowl-shaped pad of grass and feathers, located in a hole or cavity in a dead tree. The 2–5 pale blue or greenish-blue eggs are sometimes lightly spotted with red-brown.

TRACK N° **78**

Their chattering song is not heard very frequently. It is loud, varied and musical.

79 | Superb Starling
Kwezi–Maridadi

Superb Starlings are locally common, noisy and gregarious residents. Small flocks occur in thornbush and acacia country, often near towns and villages.

They forage mainly on the ground, where they walk and run after various insects, such as termites, ants, grasshoppers and beetles; they also eat fruits.

These starlings are co-operative breeders that have one or more helpers. The nest is an untidy, bulky, domed structure made of thorny twigs, with a side entrance. It is usually placed in a thorn tree and lined with dry grass and feathers. If not in a thorn tree, the starlings add thorny twigs around the nest. The female lays 2–5 glossy, bright greenish-blue eggs. Great Spotted Cuckoos parasitise their nests.

TRACK N° **79**

Superb Starlings constantly chatter among themselves; theirs is a sweet song that includes many shrill notes.

80 | Hildebrandt's Starling
Kwezi–Jangwa

Hildebrandt's Starlings are locally common residents that occur in pairs or small family groups. Gregarious, they inhabit wooded savanna and riverine areas in southern Kenya and northern Tanzania.

They forage on the ground for insects and seeds.

Their nest is a hole in a tree branch, lined with a pad of hair and fibres. However, sometimes they adopt abandoned woodpecker nests. The female usually lays 3–4 slightly glossy white eggs. Like those of the Superb Starling, Hildebrandt's Starlings' nests are parasitised by Great Spotted Cuckoos.

81 | Red-winged Starling
Kuzi mbawanyekundu

Local residents, found in pairs or small flocks on rocky hills, kopjes (in the Serengeti National Park) and cliffs, Red-winged Starlings have also adapted to life in cities and towns. They forage in open country and fly rapidly, calling repeatedly.

They hop on the ground feeding. Occasionally they perch on mammals, using them as beaters to disturb items of prey. They are omnivorous, eating carrion, insects, fruits, nectar, lizards and nestling birds.

They have a saucer-shaped nest made out of grass, rootlets and sticks, lined with grass and leaves and with a mud base. The 2–4 blue eggs have red-brown spots.

TRACK N° **80**

The song is very different from that of the similar-looking Superb Starling; it comprises deep musical churrs and nasal notes.

TRACK N° **81**

Their song is a lively, fluty series of whistled notes.

82 | Olive Thrush
Kiruwiji Kijanikijivu

Local residents, found alone or in pairs, Olive Thrushes inhabit forests, dense scrub, bush and gardens, where they become tame and confiding.

They feed on the ground, mainly on insects such as beetles, moths, grasshoppers, mantises and caterpillars; they also eat various fruits.

The nest is a large, untidy bowl made of small twigs, bark strips, rootlets and coarse grasses, bound together with mud and lined with fine grasses and plant fibres. The female lays 1–3 bluish or pale green eggs with yellowish-brown spots, blotches and streaks.

83 | White-browed Robin-Chat (Heuglin's Robin)
Kurumbiza Mchirizimweupe

Highly vocal, common residents, these robin-chats occur in riverine forests and woodlands, but avoid the interior of forests and are not found in semidesert country.

They forage on the ground for a variety of insects.

A deep cup nest is made of coarse twigs, grass and dead leaves, lined with rootlets and fine twigs, into which 2–3 olive, cream or beige eggs with red-brown markings are laid. The nests are sometimes parasitised by Red-chested Cuckoos.

TRACK N° **82**

Their usual call is a dry chattering, but in the breeding season or after heavy rain, these birds give a simple, rambling refrain, starting long before daylight, while most of the world is still asleep.

TRACK N° **83**

This songster repeats a single phrase, but the call gets louder and louder and speeds up each time. When not singing, White-browed Robin-Chats give a distinctive knocking call.

84 | Rüppell's Robin-Chat
Kurumbiza–Rupeli

Very similar in appearance to the White-browed Robin-Chat, these are birds of highland forests and gardens. Pugnacious, they chase other birds away from feeders and birdbaths.

They forage in open areas on the ground, especially in the evenings, in search of insects such as beetles, moths, caterpillars, mantises and grasshoppers.

An open cup nest is built out of rootlets, fibres, moss, decaying leaves and twigs. The female lays 2–3 glossy olive to olive-brown eggs. Nests are often parasitised by Red-chested Cuckoos.

TRACK N° **84**

No Rüppell's Robin-Chats sound alike – each individual has a great variety of calls. These robin-chats also mimic other birds so perfectly that even the most experienced birdwatchers may be fooled as to the singer's true identity.

85 | Collared Sunbird
Chozi–Mkufu

Common residents, pairs occur on forest edges, in woodlands, bush country, mangrove swamps and gardens.

Collared Sunbirds glean insects from leaves, flowers or the air. With their short bills they pierce flower bases to access the nectar. They also eat small fruits.

The nest is a flimsy, untidy, loose-knit, pouch-like pendant, with a side-top entrance and overhanging porch. Made from fine strips of fibre, dead leaves, rootlets and twigs, it is bound with spider silk, decorated with lichens and lined with fine plant down and a few feathers. The female lays 1–2 pale cream, green or blue eggs, with reddish-brown spots and streaks. The nest is often located close to a wasp or hornet nest.

TRACK N° **85**

The song is sweet, but very simple and sibilant, unlike that of other species of sunbird found in gardens.

86 | Scarlet-chested Sunbird
Chozi–Gunda

These common, conspicuous sunbirds occur in various habitats, including gardens, and often draw attention with their loud calls. They occur in pairs, sometimes in groups, at *Leonotis* flowers.

Mainly nectar feeders, they sip from flowering trees and garden flowers, but also readily take various insects.

The nest is ragged and pear shaped, with a side entrance and a porch near the top. It is built of fine fibrous grass, pieces of leaves and old spider's web, and decorated with dead leaves, grass seeds and feathers. It is lined with woolly plant down and more feathers. The female lays 2 eggs of variable colour – usually cream, tinged with green, and with sepia streaks. Klaas's and Emerald cuckoos parasitise these nests.

TRACK N° **86**

This sunbird gives some harsh calls, while its song consists of relatively short, simple, repeated phrases.

87 | Variable Sunbird
Chozi Tumbonjano

These common sunbirds occur in pairs in a variety of habitats, including gardens.

They are nectar feeders, foraging close to the ground on flowering shrubs. They also glean small insects from stems and leaves.

The nest is a suspended oval or pear shape, with a side entrance near the top. It is constructed from fine grass blades and stems, mixed with fibre rootlets and bound together with spider's web. Often, it is camouflaged with bits of dangling fibre and is lined with thistle down and a few feathers. The female lays 1–2 white or pale cream eggs that have a dusting of olive freckles.

TRACK N° **87**

Their song consists of an attractive, almost canary-like set of trills, but their other calls are sharp and explosive.

88 | White-browed Sparrow-Weaver
Korodindo Mchirizimweupe

Locally very common, gregarious residents of acacia country, White-browed Sparrow-Weavers appear to be increasing their range, and now occur, and breed, in the suburbs of Nairobi. These are very noisy birds, especially at their nesting colonies.

Usually, they are seen hopping about on the ground, feeding mainly on seeds and harvester ants.

Their nests, in groups of 20 or more, festoon acacia trees and are a feature of the habitats where they occur. They are large, untidy balls of coarse grass, with downward-facing entrances. When the birds are breeding, one entrance is closed. When not breeding, they use the nest for roosting. The female lays 2 eggs that are pink, boldly spotted with red.

TRACK N° **88**

A bird that seems to 'talk' all day. Resting birds chatter and 'squark' together endlessly.

89 | Parrot-billed (Grey-headed) Sparrow
Korobindo–Kaya (Jorowe)

These sparrows are common residents of towns and villages, but they also occur in bush country.

They feed in bare areas on the ground, taking seeds as well as insects and kitchen scraps.

An untidy nest is made of grass and feathers in a hole in a tree, or in a wall under the eaves of a house. They often also take over swallow nests. The female lays 3–5 densely marked brown eggs.

TRACK N° **89**

Theirs are not the most beautiful voices: they simply give a repeated series of dry chips, but presumably they sound good to other sparrows!

90 | Spectacled Weaver
Kwera Koojeusi

Unlike male Spectacled Weavers, females and immatures lack the black throat.

Spectacled Weavers are resident birds that usually occur in pairs in forested areas, acacia woodlands, riverine forests and rank vegetation near to streams and lakes. They are shy and skulking.

These weavers forage in the canopy, among tangled scrub and creepers, searching mainly for insects but also for small lizards, geckos, fruits and nectar. In addition, they probe crevices and flaky bark.

Both sexes build a neat, compact, unlined nest of strongly woven grass and leaf strips, with a long entrance spout that may vary from a few centimetres to up to 20cm. The female lays 2–3 white or pinkish eggs with reddish spots. Dideric Cuckoos sometimes parasitise their nests.

TRACK N° **90**

This song is a distinctive, strange skirling and chattering; it includes a series of about 6 descending notes, given from within a tangle of vines.

Males display socially by hanging from under their nests.

91 | Village (Black-headed) Weaver
Kwera Nguya

Common residents, these weavers are found in a variety of habitats, including villages.

Their main diet consists of seeds, insects and nectar.

Nests are built in crowded colonies over water or close to human habitation, which gives them some protection from snakes and other predators. The male builds a coarse, spherical nest of grass blades, with an entrance hole at the bottom. When he has completed his nest, he hangs upside down from the nest, near the entrance, and displays vigorously to any females passing by, uttering loud, zwizzing sounds and flapping his wings. When a female accepts the nest, she lines it with soft material and then lays 2–3 white or bluish-green eggs with small brown spots.

TRACK N° 91

Each bird sings a complex song, with trills, snores and chattering. A colony of nesting Village Weavers all calling at the same time can be quite deafening.

92 | Red-billed Firefinch
Bwerenda Domojekundu

Common residents, Red-billed Firefinches are found in a wide range of habitats, including towns, villages and gardens. They usually occur in pairs or family groups that always stay close together, even when flying off.

 They search the ground for small seeds.

 They build a loose, ball-like nest with a side entrance, located low down in a bush or on the ground. It is made of grass and feathers, which are also used for the lining. The female lays 3–4 whitish eggs. Village Indigobirds often parasitise these nests.

93 | Red-cheeked Cordon-bleu
Njiri Buluu Shavujekundu

Red-cheeked Cordon-bleus are common and familiar residents in a variety of habitats, including towns, villages and gardens. These birds are tame and confiding.

 Pairs or small family groups feed on the ground, eating mainly small seeds but also termites and little insects.

 The nest is ball shaped, made of grass, with a low side entrance. Usually it is located in a tree or bush where it is often very conspicuous. These cordon-bleus sometimes take over old weaver nests. The female lays 4–5 white eggs.

TRACK N° **92**

This species gives the simplest song of any firefinch in the region, comprising a few nasal chirps and chips. Village Indigobirds incorporate the song of this firefinch into their calls.

TRACK N° **93**

The song consists of high-pitched calls interspersed with rapid chattering and lisping sounds.

94 | Pin-tailed Whydah
Mzese Mweupe (Fumbwe)

Pin-tailed Whydahs are common residents in various habitats and suburban gardens, where they usually occur in small parties.

Males are greatly outnumbered by females and immature birds: they are conspicuous and pugnacious in the breeding season, chasing other birds away from feeding stations, no matter what their size. Males also have an erratic, jerky, characteristic display flight: they hover and dance in the air, directly over the females.

These whydahs feed on small seeds on the ground.

They do not build nests; instead, they parasitise those of various waxbills, especially the Common Waxbill, laying their white eggs in the host's nest.

95 | Village Indigobird
Kitongo Domojekundu

These indigobirds are common residents that occur in a wide variety of habitats, including gardens.

Their diet consists of small seeds gleaned from the ground.

They do not build nests. Rather, they parasitise those of Red-billed Firefinches, and their eggs match those of their hosts.

TRACK N° 94
Single birds station themselves on the tops of small trees and bushes, chirping away in the hope of attracting a passing female.

TRACK N° 95
Males sing from the same post for most of the day, every day, occasionally flying off to feed, but quickly returning and singing exuberantly.

59

Nigel Dennis/IOA

96 | African Pied Wagtail
Kiluwiluwi Majumba

Tame and confiding birds, African Pied Wagtails may be solitary, or occur in pairs, and are found throughout the region. They are often common in towns and villages and near water. Occasionally, hundreds of these birds gather together at communal roosts. Local people believe that the Pied Wagtails in their villages bring them luck.

These birds walk and run along the ground, continually wagging their tails, and snatching up various insects such as dragonflies, butterflies, moths, small beetles, termites and ants. Occasionally, they take short flights to catch flying insects.

The nest, a rough, bulky cup, is built of soft, dry grass and lined with fine grass, hair and soft feathers. It is usually located in a niche in a river bank, on a building or on a boat. The 3–4 white eggs have pale grey flecks. Red-chested and Dideric cuckoos often parasitise these nests.

TRACK N° **96**

Their song is a long, beautiful, varied and warbling refrain, often heard early in the morning. They call frequently, particularly in flight, giving a dry 'chrip' and also give a simple 'siu siu siu–si si si si'.

97 | Yellow-throated Longclaw
Tokeeo Koomanjano

98 | African Citril
Chiruku Mdogo

 Common local residents, Yellow-throated Longclaws occur singly or in pairs in grasslands, open bush country and cultivated areas. Their distinctive jerky flight is characterised by gliding, interspersed with short periods of flapping. They get their name from the extremely long hind claw on each foot, which enables them to walk and run easily over tussocky grass. When the grass is wet, these birds sun themselves on termite mounds or bushes.

 Pairs often forage on the ground, taking long strides and eating insect larvae, grasshoppers, beetles and butterflies.

 A deep cup nest of grass stems and blades, lined with fine rootlets and fibres, is placed against a tussock or low bush. The female lays 2–4 grey-white eggs, with fine brown spots and streaks.

 African Citrils are common, and are usually found in pairs or small flocks along forest edges, in acacia country or in cultivated areas.

 They feed on seeds, sometimes among roadside weeds, and also occasionally glean insects from grass stems and leaves.

 They build a small, neat cup nest constructed from dry grass and rootlets, decorated with spider's web and cocoons, and lined with plant down. They lay 2–3 dull white or cream eggs with reddish spots and blotches.

TRACK N° **97**

A set of identical sweet notes is given repeatedly from the top of a bush or in flight. The song is more varied, with fluty and nasal notes.

TRACK N° **98**

African Citrils are sweet, but fast, singers, and their song is heard well into the morning. Their call, given mainly in the morning, comprises rising and falling minor notes, and may lead into the complete song.

99 | Brimstone Canary
Chiruku Manjano

Common, widespread, upland residents of wooded grasslands and cultivated areas, Brimstone Canaries occur singly or in pairs and occasionally in small family parties. They have a distinctive large bill.

These canaries forage on the ground and in bushes for seeds, fruits and the young shoots and buds of trees. They are able to crack open large seeds, using their heavy bills.

The nest is a cup of grass and weeds, lined with soft, fine grass fibres and woolly down. The 2–4 pale green eggs have dark brown or black blemishes and spots.

100 | Streaky Seedeater
Mpasuambegu Michirizi

Streaky Seedeaters are common, widespread residents of the East African highlands. They inhabit forest edges, moorlands, cultivated areas and gardens.

Small seeds, taken on the ground or directly from seed heads, form their main diet. They also eat small fruits and insects and sip nectar from flowers.

A cup nest is built out of rootlets, twigs, grass and moss, and is lined with hair and feathers. Usually it is located low in a bush or among creepers. The 3–4 creamish or greenish-white eggs are marked with dark brown scrawls and speckles.

TRACK N° **99**
A very simple, burry call is given from an exposed perch. However, the song is much more attractive and varied.

TRACK N° **100**
Their most common calls are a buzzy 'tzreep' and a 'swizyu'; the song is heard only in the breeding season and is a very attractive and varied medley of sweet notes and trills.

REFERENCES

Richards, D. 1995. *A Photographic Guide to Birds of East Africa*, 3rd edition. New Holland, London.

Stevenson, T. & Fanshawe, J. 2002. *Field Guide to the Birds of East Africa*. T. & A.D. Poyser, London.

Zimmerman, D.A., Turner, D.A. & Pearson, D.J. 1996. *Birds of Kenya and Northern Tanzania*. Russel Friedman Books, South Africa.

RECOMMENDED READING

Cambell, B. & Lack, E. 1985. *A Dictionary of Birds*. T. & A.D. Poyser, London.

Loon, R. & H. 2005. *Birds – the Inside Story*. Struik Publishers, South Africa.

Lederer, R. & Burr, C. 2014. *Latin for Bird Watchers*. Struik Nature, South Africa.

Scopus. 1977–2015. *Journal of the Ornithological Sub-committee of the East African Natural History Society*.

Mainly nectar feeders, Scarlet-chested Sunbirds sip from flowering trees and garden flowers.

INDEX